Landmarks from the Past

Gillian Clegg

Wayland

Landmarks from the Past

Editors: Margot Richardson/William Wharfe
Designer: Joyce Chester

Front cover: *main picture* Castlerigg stone circle, Cumbria; *top left* milestone, near Halifax, West Yorkshire; *top middle* Long Man hill figure, Wilmington, East Sussex; *top right* Halnaker windmill, West Sussex.
Back cover: Gillian Clegg.
Title page: Maiden Castle, Dorset; see page 14.

Picture Acknowledgements
The publishers gratefully acknowledge the permission of the following to use their photographs as illustrations in this book: English Heritage 11 (Judith Dobie), 28 (Skyscan); Robert Estall *cover* top middle (Malcolm Aird), 17, 26, 31; Mary Evans Picture Library 19 (C.B. Newhouse), 22 (J.C. Bourne); Eye Ubiquitous *cover* top left (Dorothy Burrows), 13 (D. Gill), 15 (Douglas Kerr), 18 (J. Shaw), 20 (M.J. Frankland), 21 (Michael Reed), 23 (Paul Seheult), 27 (Tom Curtis), 29 (Michael Reed), 30 (Roger Chester), 34 (Hugh Rooney), 35 (Dorothy Burrows), 40 (Paul Seheult), 41; Manunair 6 (G.D.B. Jones), 24 (K. Maude), 25 (G.D.B. Jones); Michael Holford 10; Skyscan Balloon Photography 1, 14, 33, 37, 39; Zefa *cover* main picture and top right, 4, 5 (P.J. Sharpe), 9 (Karl E. Deckart), 32, 38 (G. Mabbs).
The map on page 7 was reproduced from the 1992 Ordnance Survey 1:50,000 Landranger Hexham & Haltwhistle (No 87) map with the permission of the Controller of Her Majesty's Stationery Office © Crown copyright.
Artwork was supplied by: Mark Peppé 8; Peter Dennis 12, 36; John James 16.
The map on page 3 was drawn by Peter Bull.
Symbols at the top corners of each page were drawn by John Yates.

First published in 1994 by
Wayland (Publishers) Ltd
61 Western Road, Hove
East Sussex BN3 1JD, England

© Copyright 1994 Wayland (Publishers) Limited

British Library Cataloguing in Publication Data

Clegg, Gillian
Landmarks from the Past
I. Title
941

ISBN 0 7502 0892 9

Typeset in the UK by Dorchester Typesetting Group Ltd
Printed and bound in Great Britain by B.P.C.C. Paulton Books

Contents

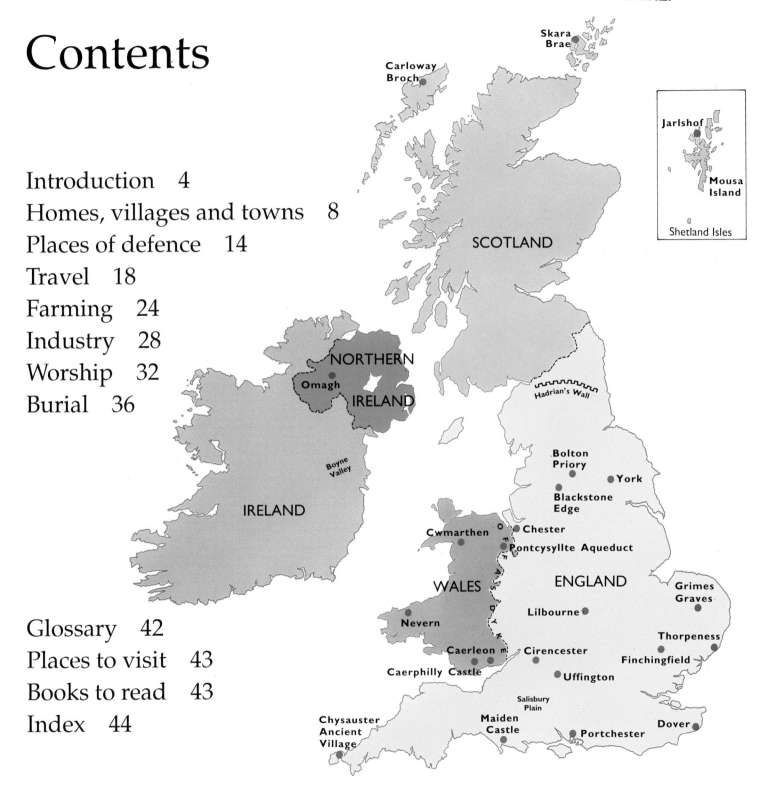

This map shows the sites of places to visit (see page 43) and the landmarks illustrated in photos throughout the book.

Introduction

People have lived in Britain for over 400,000 years and they have left behind, in the landscape, plenty of evidence of their presence.

Much of this is under the ground and can only be recovered by archaeological excavation; some is invisible on the surface of the land and can only be seen from the air. However, there are still many remains from earlier times you can see in your own area, or as you travel around.

This book should help you recognize the marks on the land made by people in the past. It explains why they were made and what they were used for.

From very early times people have grown crops, cut down trees, mined for minerals, quarried for stone, and built buildings. In later times people have also used wind, water and steam to power machinery; they have constructed roads, railways and canals. All these activities have left their marks on the land.

Many of the marks are just lumps and bumps in the ground. These could be the remains of mounds under which people buried their dead, banks used to mark a boundary, or to

▲ Silbury Hill, in Wiltshire, is one of the largest 'bumps' in the landscape. It was put up in prehistoric times but nobody knows what it was for. Perhaps it covered the grave of a very important person.

prevent attacks from enemies. They could be mounds on which castles or windmills once stood, or they could be covering deserted buildings. It takes a bit of practice to know what the different lumps and bumps mean and to distinguish artificial lumps from natural features, such as the small hills you find in, for example, the Lake District and Somerset.

There are also depressions in the ground, often filled with water. Although some are natural or man-made ponds and lakes, others are what's left of old quarries or mines.

Stones are another common landmark. Early people used gigantic stones to make their burial mounds and temples. Later stone marks include walls, castles, churches, crosses, milestones and gravestones. Some strange stone formations, though, were caused by glaciers in the Ice Age, or by the action of the sea. These are sometimes confused with marks left by people.

What archaeology can tell us

Archaeologists can find other marks on the ground. They dig down through the soil, layer by layer, to discover how people used to live. Soil builds up over old sites and if the site has been in use for hundreds of years, there will be many layers of remains on top of each other. The oldest layers are at the bottom and the newest at the top.

Archaeologists can uncover old walls, and they can work out the shape of early buildings from the dark stains left in the soil where posts were put up. (Wooden posts rot away but leave a dark mark behind, showing where they were.) The soil in old ditches and rubbish pits is also a different colour, so archaeologists can see where these were. Some of the most important things archaeologists find come from rubbish pits! Hearths of fires show up as charcoal stains in the ground, and shallow pits sometimes reveal graves containing skeletons.

▼ An archaeological excavation in Chester, Cheshire, a town which dates back to the Roman period. Archaeologists find the remains of buildings, bones, tools, weapons, jewellery, coins, pottery, traces of plants and insects. These help to date the site and show how people lived at that time.

Periods in history

Archaeologists and historians divide the time people have lived in Britain into different periods:

Palaeolithic: 1,000,000 – 10,000 BC
The first people came to live in Britain. They probably came from Europe, as Britain was connected to the European continent at this time. Palaeolithic people made simple tools of wood and stone. They were nomadic, following around the animals they hunted for food. The Ice Age occurred during this period.

Mesolithic: 10,000 – 4,000 BC
People made more complicated tools than their Palaeolithic ancestors (using stone, wood and bone); but they were still nomadic hunters and gatherers.

Neolithic: 4,000 – 2,500 BC
People knew how to cultivate wild cereal grasses for food and how to domesticate and herd the animals their Mesolithic ancestors had hunted. This meant they could live in one place all the time, and build more permanent homes.

Bronze Age: 2,500 – 600 BC
People learnt how to make tools from the metal bronze, a combination of copper and tin.

Iron Age: 600 BC – AD 43
Iron largely replaced bronze as the metal used for weapons and tools. (Iron is stronger than bronze.)

Roman: AD 43 – 410
The years when Britain was part of the Roman Empire.

Saxon: 410 – 1066
Saxons from Germany and other people, such as the Vikings from Scandinavia, settled in Britain.

Medieval (also known as the Middle Ages): 1066 – 1485
The Saxons were defeated by Norman invaders from northern France in 1066. England was then ruled by a Norman king (William I) and his barons. For the next 400 years England (and later Wales) was run on a feudal system – with peasants at the bottom ruled by lords of the manor, who were, in turn, ruled by the barons, and the king.

Later times are generally described in centuries. For example, the seventeenth century refers to the hundred years leading up to the century number: from 1600 to 1699.

What can be seen from the air

Photographs taken from the air often show the location of earthworks (such as mounds, banks and ditches) and old buildings from crop marks. When the weather is very dry, crops grow better over old pits and ditches, which stay damp, and less well over old walls where the soil is dryer. Photographs taken at the right time of year can show the perfect outline of an old building or other things which lie below the ground, but which cannot be seen from ground level.

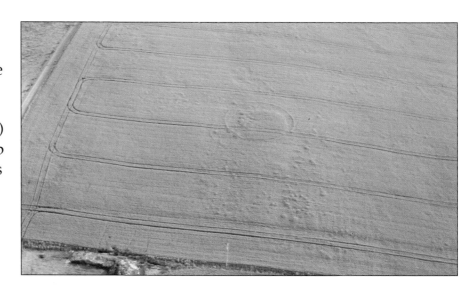

▲ These round crop marks, invisible from the ground, show the position of an ancient hut and its rubbish pits.

6

How to use maps

To start looking for old marks on the land, it is a great help to have a good map. Large-scale maps – which show a small number of kilometres to each centimetre on the map – are best, because they contain the most detail. The most detailed maps available are the Ordnance Survey Pathfinder and Landranger series.

▼ This part of an Ordnance Survey Landranger map for Northumberland shows Roman roads, camps and forts, an old castle, and a tumulus – a prehistoric burial mound.

Pathfinder maps are 4 cm to 1 km in scale (1:25,000). Landranger maps are 2 cm to 1 km (1:50,000).

At the beginning or on the edge of the map you will find a guide to the symbols the map uses to show different things. Unfortunately, different maps use different symbols, but a common symbol is a large red M meaning a monument. Some maps write the names of ancient things in gothic letters like this: Abbey. Some use a different colour ink to name ancient sites.

Project

Making a map
Make a map of landmarks from the past in your area.

1 Find a large-scale Ordnance Survey map, or a good road map, of your suburb, village or town. Many public libraries keep maps of this sort, if you don't have one at home.
2 Work out where your house is on the map. Look at the area of about 5 km (or, in a city, 2 km) in every direction from your house.
3 On a piece of tracing paper, make a map of any landmarks near your home. These could be churches, graveyards, old houses, paths, etc.
   If you live in or near the country, are there any monuments, historic sites, Roman roads or disused railway lines nearby?
4 Investigate the area on foot, noting down anything which is not marked on the printed map, but which is evidence of the past. For example, are there any old post boxes or telephone boxes in the streets near your house?
5 Once you have drawn your local map, work out which is the oldest landmark.
6 Write down which landmarks you think are the most interesting, and why.

Homes, villages and towns

The first homes were little more than simple shelters and caves. Then huts were built and homes gradually became larger and more comfortable. Small groups of people living in the same place grew into the villages and towns we know today.

The first people to live in the British Isles arrived approximately 440,000 years ago, during the last Ice Age (which occurred during the Palaeolithic period). The climate wasn't always cold in the Ice Age, though. There were warm spells, lasting thousands of years, when animals such as elephants, lions, hippopotamuses and rhinoceroses roamed the country.

Caves

There were times when Britain was as cold as the Arctic is today. During these periods, people would shelter in the mouths of caves or under overhanging rocks. The animals in Britain then included bison, mammoth, horse and reindeer, and bones that have been found in caves tell us that early people hunted and ate these animals.

Caves used by early people that can still be seen today are Kent's Cavern, near Torquay in Devon; Paviland Cave, at Gower in Glamorgan; and five caves on the Cresswell Crags in Derbyshire.

Caves were not only used in the cold Palaeolithic period. Some people, such as hermits in the medieval period, have always preferred them to houses. Well-known caves you can visit are Wookey Hole in Somerset, which was lived in during prehistoric and Roman times; and the cave in Knaresborough, Yorkshire, which was occupied in the fifteenth century by Mother Shipton, who predicted the invention of motor cars and aeroplanes.

Huts

The people of the Palaeolithic and Mesolithic periods were hunters. Because they needed to follow the animal herds, they were always on the move and only put up

▼ Very old bones, found in caves, suggest that some people lived there during the Ice Age.

temporary huts, made of branches, with roofs made of thatch or animal skin. Sometimes they lived in hollow scoops in the ground covered by branches, bracken or turves.

By 4000 BC, people had learnt to farm, so they could live in one place all the time. Neolithic, Bronze Age and Iron Age people usually lived in round or rectangular huts. These were normally made by weaving branches together and filling the holes between the branches with clay to make a wall. Since wood decays, the huts themselves no longer survive, but archaeologists recognize them on excavations from the stains in the soil left by the posts that supported the walls and roof. Examples of how these wooden huts may have looked can be seen in some open-air museums: the Ulster History Park at Omagh, County Tyrone, has rebuilt Neolithic huts, and there are Iron Age huts at Butser Hill, near Petersfield in Hampshire, which is a recreated Iron Age farm.

In hilly areas, homes were built in stone, which is lucky for us as some still survive today. The best

▲ Neolithic people lived in these stone huts at Skara Brae. As there were no trees there, the furniture was also made of stone.

examples of very early (Neolithic) stone huts are in the Orkney Islands, Scotland. Those at Skara Brae are well worth visiting. Very ruined remains of Neolithic stone huts can also be seen in England, for example at Carn Brae, near Redruth in Cornwall.

Later (Bronze Age and Iron Age) stone huts can be found in Cornwall, Devon, Yorkshire, Wales and Scotland. Good examples are Grimspound on Dartmoor, where there are several huts surrounded by a circular wall, and Jarlshof in the Shetland Isles. In Jarlshof, the most unusual remains are the wheelhouses. These are circular huts divided by walls forming shapes like segments in an orange. Wheelhouses were built in the Iron Age, and are only found in Scotland.

Iron Age huts can also be seen at Chysauster near Penzance, and Carn Euny, Cornwall. At both these places there are underground passages with rooms leading off them. These are called *souterrains* or *fogous*. Nobody knows what they were used for.

Perhaps they were for storing food, for sheltering animals, or they might have been where people could hide in times of trouble.

Early Saxon huts were a bit like a tent: rectangular, with a post at either end and a sunken floor. None of these survive intact today, but reconstructed Saxon huts can be seen at West Stow in Suffolk. Many Viking huts were shaped like a boat.

Houses

The first really grand houses in Britain were built in the Roman period. Rich people owned large estates of many farms, and the landowner's home, or villa, in the countryside was often modelled on houses in Italy. These had a number of rooms connected by a covered corridor, or arranged around a courtyard.

Some of these villas were very luxurious with bathrooms, central heating, and floors decorated with mosaics (patterns made with tiny squares of coloured stone). A visit to the Roman villas at Lullingstone in Kent, Bignor and Fishbourne Palace in Sussex and

▲ Part of the mosaic floor from a Roman house in Cirencester. In Roman times, mosaic floors were a status symbol. Firms of mosaic artists created the designs, which could be patterns, or pictures, often taken from classical stories.

Chedworth in Gloucestershire shows how sophisticated Roman society must have been. Most homes didn't have bathrooms and central heating again until this century.

Many of the houses lived in by richer people in the medieval period were surrounded by a moat, a wide, water-filled ditch. Early moats were oval and were intended to keep enemies out. Later moats were square or rectangular and not built for defence, but as a sign of the owner's importance. Moats were probably also used for storing water and for keeping fish.

Villages

From the earliest times, groups of huts were clustered together and often surrounded by a bank of earth or a wall for protection against attack. What is thought to be the oldest village street in Britain is in Chysauster Ancient Village (see page 9). It was lived in during the Iron Age and Roman periods. It was excavated some years ago and is now open to the public.

Many of today's villages probably date from the twelfth century AD or earlier. By this time, the large farming estates of Roman times had been broken up into smaller units controlled by a lord of the manor.

Although villages have changed over the years, many still have remains of their medieval past. These are the signs to look for: an old church near the centre of the village; the lord's manor house or castle; a pump or well for drinking water; a village green where the villagers would graze their animals, often with a pond. There are so many old villages that there is bound to be a good example somewhere near where you live. Very pretty old villages are Corfe Castle, Dorset; Finchingfield, Essex; Weobley near Hereford; and Cartmel, Cumbria.

▼ This is what the ancient village of Chysauster in Cornwall probably looked like in Iron Age times. It had four pairs of houses, all opening on to the village street.

Landmarks from the Past

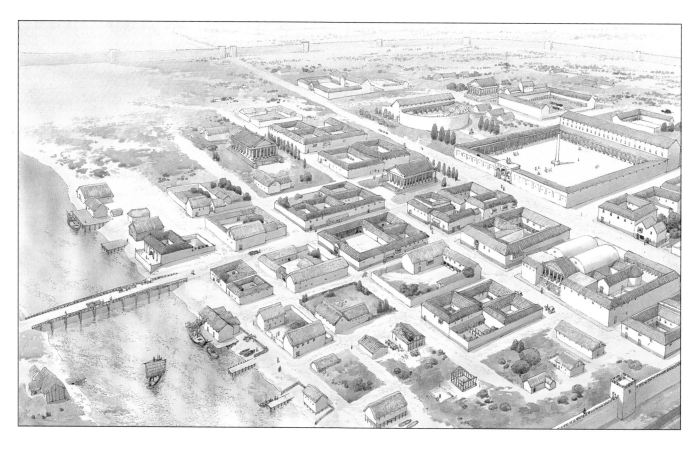

▲ Roman towns were well planned, in a square pattern, with the most important buildings usually in the centre of the town. Can you find the market place, the temples and the theatre?

Deserted villages

Over the years many villages became smaller, due to a combination of changes in the weather, the death of huge numbers of people in the plagues of the fourteenth century, and changing methods of farming. Some villages were abandoned altogether.

You can often see their remains in aerial photos and sometimes on the ground. If you see a church (possibly ruined) standing on its own, look for fields nearby with lots of grassy humps. These could mark the position of the original buildings. Nettles grow well on old rubbish pits, so see if there are patches of nettles in certain areas. There might also be stretches of water which could be the remains of moats or ponds.

Famous deserted villages are Wharram Percy in Yorkshire, and Quarrendon in Buckinghamshire.

Towns

The Romans were the first people to build towns in Britain. Roman towns were laid out like a giant chessboard with streets crossing each other at right angles. Towns were protected by walls, with large gates for entry, which were shut at night. At the centre of the town were the basilica (the town hall and law courts) and the forum (market-place). There would also have been public baths and perhaps a theatre.

Towns and cities which were originally Roman include Chichester, Colchester, Lincoln, Gloucester, York and London. Evidence of their Roman past often turns up when streets are widened or new buildings put up. The town of St Albans was built right beside the Roman town of Verulamium, and so is a good place to see Roman remains.

In Saxon times, people seem to have preferred living in villages. The Roman towns appear to have been abandoned and not lived in again until around the tenth century or later. Some villages grew into towns, and other new towns were built.

Early towns were defended by ditches and earth banks. Some of these can still be seen at Wareham, in Dorset. Most of the banks and ditches were replaced later by stout stone walls. As towns expanded they grew outside the walls, which were often pulled down. But you can still see medieval walls today at places like Chester, Chichester and York. All early towns would have had a market, so see if you can still see the old market-place and market cross.

▶ For protection against enemies, medieval towns were enclosed by walls. You could only enter the town through gates which were shut at night. In the city of York, the old wall and its four gates are still standing. You can walk around the city on top of the wall.

Places of defence

There have always been enemies, whether a neighbouring tribe or invaders from overseas. Many different types of fortification have been built to keep people safe.

Causewayed camps

Neolithic farmers built huge enclosures ringed by banks and ditches. The banks had gaps for entrances. These causewayed enclosures might have protected huts where people lived, but they seem to have been used for other purposes too: places where people met, and where cattle were kept or killed. The remains of causewayed enclosures can be seen on Knap Hill and Windmill Hill, both in Wiltshire. You will have to look carefully for these – the banks are now very low and the ditches are shallow.

Hillforts

By the time of the Iron Age, Britain was split up between many different tribes who often fought each other. For protection against raids, groups of huts were surrounded by huge banks and ditches on the top of hills.

The earliest hillforts had just one bank (rampart), but later hillforts often had several ramparts. Hillforts are a very distinctive feature on the landscape and many can still be seen, especially on hills in south and west England. Good examples are Maiden Castle in Dorset, and Cissbury in Sussex.

To identify a hillfort, look for the tops of hills which are a different shape from the hills around (not so smooth) and hills which appear to go up in a number of ridges.

▼ The hillfort at Maiden Castle, Dorset. It was built during the Iron Age, with rows of banks and ditches to make attacks difficult.

Forts

Instead of hillforts, the Iron Age people in Scotland and Wales built small circular stone forts for defence. (An example is Rahoy, on Loch Teacuis in Argyll.) In the north of Scotland and the islands, chiefs defended their homes with tall circular towers. These are called brochs and many can still be seen. The best example is on Mousa Island in the Shetland Isles.

The Romans, who invaded Britain in AD 43, built forts as permanent bases for the army. There were lines of forts in Wales,

▶ The remains of Carloway Broch in Lewis, Western Isles. Originally, it would have been about 10 m tall.

the north of England and southern and eastern Scotland. The forts, large and small, were all of a similar design: rectangular with rounded corners, like a playing card. Caerleon in Gwent, designed to hold over 5,000 soldiers, is one of the best examples, and Housesteads on Hadrian's Wall in Northumberland is worth a visit – you can still see the soldiers' communal lavatories! The Lunt fort, near Coventry, is a reconstructed Roman fort.

About 200 years later, the Romans put up a new type of fort to defend the coast of England from invasions by the Saxons. These forts had turrets and strong towers (called bastions) protruding from the walls. Known as Saxon shore forts, they were built along the coast from Norfolk to Hampshire. The fort in Portchester, Hampshire, gives a good idea of what they were like. Similar forts were built along the Welsh coast to keep out Irish pirates.

Much later, in about 1800, two-storey round towers were put up around the south and east coasts of England and around Dublin in Ireland, as defences against the French, who were planning to invade Britain. These Martello towers contained a large gun that swivelled around. Martello towers that have been preserved include those in Dublin, and in Pevensey and Eastbourne, Sussex. You can still see the remains of other Martello towers, although often they are no more than stumps.

Landmarks from the Past

Signal stations

The Romans also built watchtowers and signal stations so that the forts could be warned of approaching raiders. There was a line of these towers to the west of Perth in Scotland (a well-preserved example is Fendoch). The Romans also built stone towers along the cliffs of the Yorkshire coast to watch for invaders or pirates.

▼ A typical motte and bailey castle from the Norman period. Although the wooden buildings would have long since rotted away, many motte mounds can be seen in the landscape (see page 25).

Castles

The Normans, who conquered England in 1066, built castles to protect themselves from attacks by the English. The first castles consisted of a motte and bailey. The motte was a mound made by digging a circular ditch and piling up the soil in the centre. The mound was flattened on the top and surrounded by a fence. A wooden watch tower was built on the mound. The bailey was an area next to it, protected by a ditch and bank, which contained the wooden buildings where the owner and his soldiers lived. There are remains of motte and bailey castles all over Britain (particularly on the border between England and Wales). The wooden buildings haven't survived, so often all you can see is the motte, and if this is in country fields it can be confused with a Bronze Age burial mound (see

Keep

Motte

Bailey

Drawbridge

page 38). Mountfichet Castle near Stansted, Essex, is a reconstructed motte and bailey castle. Stone castles have been built on some mottes, for example Cardiff Castle and Windsor Castle.

Later, castles were built in stone with strong walls and towers, often surrounded by a moat (don't muddle this with a motte). The entrance to the castle was by a drawbridge: a bridge across the moat which could be raised to prevent people getting into the castle. Inside the walls were the living quarters, called the keep.

There are stone castles all over Britain. Good examples of castles that date from the medieval period are Bodiam in Sussex, Bamburgh in Northumberland and Harlech in Wales.

Some castles of a completely different shape – squat and very round –

▲ Caerphilly Castle, Wales, was built in the thirteenth century. Cromwell's troops tried to blow it up with gunpowder during the Civil War (1642–48) which is why the tower on the left is leaning.

were built in the sixteenth century to defend the shores of Britain against the French. Their round walls were much better for deflecting cannon-balls than the rectangular walls of most medieval castles. Deal Castle in Kent is a good example of this type.

Travel

How did people get around? At first they walked or rode along tracks, or went by boat along rivers. Roads, canals and railways were built later to make it easier and quicker both to travel and to take goods from place to place.

Roads

People have been trading goods with each other since prehistoric times, so tracks from place to place can be very old. Some ancient tracks eventually became the roads we use today, but others, like sections of the Icknield Way, which ran from Norfolk to Wiltshire, and the prehistoric Jurassic Way from Lincolnshire to Dorset, just remain as paths.

Where the land was wet and marshy, wooden planks were laid on the ground, and archaeologists have found the wooden remains of very early roads in Somerset, preserved by the water that covered them when they went out of use.

The Romans built an efficient main-road system in Britain, to enable soldiers and other people to get around the country quickly. Roman roads were usually very wide (as much as 15 metres) with drainage ditches on either side. Gravel or stone was laid on the surface so that the road could be used in all weathers. Although Roman roads are famous for being straight, they are not so much one straight line, but more a series of straight lines, as Roman engineers avoided obstacles and boggy land.

We drive along many stretches of Roman road today. Some of the present A1 is on the line of Ermine Street, the main Roman road from London to York, and sections of the A46 in the Midlands are on the line of the Roman road from Exeter to Lincoln, which was called the Fosse Way.

◄ Roman roads were so well made that people continued to use them for many centuries after the Romans left Britain. These remains of a Roman road can be seen at Blackstone Edge on the border between Lancashire and Yorkshire.

You can see original stretches of Roman roads in some places, for example on Wheeldale Moor in North Yorkshire, and on the Blackstone Edge, near Littleborough in Lancashire.

In Saxon and medieval times, minor lanes and roads linked village to village, and village to town, where villagers took their animals, vegetables and other products to sell at the market.

You sometimes come across the remains of an old lane or track sunk 6 metres or so below the ground, with trees on either side. These holloways, as they are called, are often medieval or earlier lanes which have been worn down by centuries of use.

Roads were not very well looked after during the medieval period and in later years, which made travelling difficult. In the eighteenth century, companies called turnpike trusts were set up to look after some roads and to build new ones which would be more suitable for the fast, horse-drawn coaches in which people then travelled around. The turnpike trusts raised the

▲ In the eighteenth and nineteenth centuries people had to pay to use main roads. Here, the horseman has woken up the toll collector to open the gate. Animals and carts, as well as people, had to be paid for. The toll board on the left shows how much was paid for each.

money for building and mending the roads by charging people for using them. The roads would have a turnpike gate across the entrance and a toll-house where people paid money to use the road. Some toll-houses can still be seen, such as Sudborough toll-house on the A6116 in Northampton and Botley toll-house on the A3051 in Hampshire.

Other new – and often very straight – roads were built when changes were made to the way people farmed in the eighteenth and nineteenth centuries (see page 25). These enclosure roads, as they are known, can often be recognized by their hedges, which are exactly parallel to each other.

Look for early milestones by the sides of roads. Milestones show the distance to and from the nearest towns. The Romans had milestones every thousand paces, and milestones were required by law on British roads in the eighteenth century. Many of these can still be seen. One of the earliest (1727) is at Trumpington, Cambridge.

Fords and bridges

People first crossed rivers at fords: places where the river was shallow. There were many fords in Britain, as you can tell from the large number of places with names ending in 'ford' (such as Stamford, Ashford). Fords were gradually replaced by bridges. Early wooden bridges have not survived, but you can still see some simple, early stone bridges such as the Tarr Steps over the River Barle on Exmoor and the Post Bridge on Dartmoor.

From the thirteenth century, wooden bridges were replaced by stone ones. Look out for packhorse bridges, which usually have just a single, high arch over a river and are very narrow. Later in the medieval period, every

▲ An ancient packhorse bridge at Wycoller, Colne, in Lancashire. It is so narrow that only one horse would be able to go over it at a time. See how the stones are worn down by centuries of use.

bridge had its own cross and many had chapels for blessing travellers. The chapels at St Ives, Cambridgeshire, Wakefield, Yorkshire and Bradford-on-Avon, Wiltshire, still survive.

The first bridge in the world to be made of cast iron was put up at a place now called Ironbridge, in Shropshire, in 1779 – and it's still there. The use of materials like iron and concrete enabled bridges to span wider stretches of water and to be built in different ways. The Clifton 'Suspension' bridge in Bristol, Avon, opened in 1864, is an early example of new engineering methods.

Canals

People have always used rivers to get from place to place and to transport the goods they traded. But rivers are not very straight, and don't necessarily go where you want them to. The problem was solved by digging artificial waterways called canals. The first canals were probably made by the Romans, such as the Fossdyke linking the rivers Trent and Witham in Lincolnshire. Most canals, though, were cut between 1760 and 1850. There was more industry in Britain by this time, and canals were mainly used to transport coal and other materials from mines to factories, and goods from factories to towns and ports.

Canals have another function too – to drain water from marshy land – which is why there are so many canals in the fenlands around Lincolnshire and Norfolk.

Canals involved complicated engineering works. To remain level in areas where there are hills and valleys they often go through long tunnels, and over big aqueducts: high bridges which carry water.

A well-preserved aqueduct is Pontcysyllte in Clwyd, Wales. Locks (gates to allow boats to move from one level of water to another) had to be built. The first canal boats were pulled by men, then horses, walking along the towpath beside the canal.

▼ The Pontcysyllte aqueduct in Clwyd, Wales, which carries the Llangollen canal over the River Dee. It was built in 1805 and is nearly 39 m above the river.

Landmarks from the Past

After railways were developed, canals were no longer so important since railways can take goods from place to place more quickly. Many canals went out of use altogether. If you see a wide, damp ditch running in a fairly straight line it may well be the remains of an old canal. You can still see old canals in cities, for example the Manchester Ship Canal, and the Grand Union Canal in north London. There is also a canal museum at Stoke Bruerne near Towcester in Northamptonshire.

Railways

The earliest railway track was laid in Nottinghamshire in 1597. The first railways had wooden tracks and were pulled by horses. They were mainly used to transport coal from mines to rivers or the sea, where the coal was loaded on to ships. When locomotives powered by steam were invented at the beginning of the nineteenth century, railways with steel tracks were built all over the country, mainly between 1830 and 1850.

The building of railways was a very important event in British history, and made many changes to the wealth of the country and its way

▼ Blasting rocks at Linslade, Bedfordshire, to build the railway from London to Birmingham in 1837.

▲ This lawn covers an old railway line, and the station buildings (Barcombe Mills, Sussex) are now a restaurant. Many British railway lines were closed in the 1960s.

of life. Not only did the railways carry goods speedily to and from mines and factories, but they also carried people. Long-distance travel by coach and horses went out of fashion and many of the main roads were not used very much again until the arrival of the motor car in the twentieth century.

As railways can't climb steep hills, building railway lines was very complicated. Vast mounds of earth were dug to make embankments, long tunnels to take the lines through hills, and viaducts to take the lines on a bridge over valleys and rivers.

In the 1960s, with more and more people and goods travelling by road, many railway lines were closed, their metal rails removed and the railway stations turned into houses. You can still see where many of these railways ran and their straight, level tracks are pleasant places to go walking or cycling.

Some short lengths of railway line have been restored so that people can experience riding on an old train pulled by a steam engine. Steam railways include the Bluebell Railway in Sussex and the Severn Valley Railway in Shropshire.

23

Farming

Crops have been grown and animals kept for their meat, milk and skins since people learnt to farm 6,000 years ago. Farming has left some interesting marks on the land.

In Neolithic times, much of Britain was covered by thick forests. The first farmers probably had to spend many hours clearing away the trees before they could grow their crops. At first they dug the land with simple digging sticks. The first ploughs were very light and didn't turn the earth over. Heavier ploughs, pulled by oxen, were introduced in the Iron Age, which meant that even hard, rocky soil could be used to grow crops.

Celtic fields

The earliest fields were small, often less than half a hectare or about half the size of a football pitch. They were divided from each other by banks of earth or stone. Pottery found in the banks (perhaps the bowls and cups used by the farmers) shows that they date from the Bronze Age or even earlier. The outlines of these Celtic fields can be seen on Dartmoor and on the chalk downs of southern Britain such as Fyfield Down in Dorset.

Strip lynchets

The slopes of some hills appear to be terraced; that is, to consist of a series of ridges following the contours of the hill. This is the result of ploughing, probably in medieval times: ploughing pushed the soil downhill where it was piled into a bank (lynchet) at the edge of each strip.

▼ The long ridges on the hill in the middle distance are strip lynchets. Ploughing these hill terraces allowed farmers to increase the amount of crops they could grow. Some narrower ridges on hills, however, are just tracks made by sheep.

Ridge and furrow

In the medieval period, villages had large open fields. These were divided into strips; there were several hundred strips to a field. Villagers cultivated their own strips. The way these strips were ploughed has left an obvious pattern on the land. As the plough could only turn to the right, it was necessary to plough the strip up and down and round and round several times, starting in the middle. This meant the soil was heaped up towards the centre where it formed a

ridge, separated from the ridge of the next strip by a lower furrow.

You can still see a clear ridge and furrow pattern in many places on the ground, particularly in the Midlands, coastal parts of Yorkshire and on the border of England and Wales. Imagine the pattern of a corrugated iron roof, and look for a similar effect in the landscape.

▲ This deserted village, Lilbourne, near Rugby in Warwickshire, is surrounded by the ridge and furrow pattern of medieval ploughing. The two mounds in the centre are the remains of a motte and bailey castle.

Enclosed fields

After the medieval period, the large, open fields were gradually split up. This happened slowly at first, but between 1740 and 1850 landowners got permission to enclose fields by acts of Parliament. Smaller fields allowed farming to become more scientific, with the rotation of crops and pasture. However, many people lost their land, and their means of making a living, as a result. New farmhouses and roads were built and the landscape became the chessboard pattern we know today of small, squarish fields with hedges or stone walls.

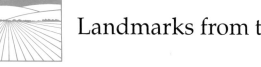

Landmarks from the Past

Boundary marks

From the prehistoric period onwards, the boundaries between one group of people and another were often marked by banks and ditches. The larger of these banks and ditches are known as dykes and many were obviously meant to protect one community from its neighbours. Iron Age people constructed dykes, such as the Devil's Dyke in Hertfordshire, to defend themselves from raids by other tribes; the Romans built them against the Saxon invaders (Wandsdyke, Wiltshire). The most famous dyke is Offa's Dyke, which runs from near Prestatyn in north Wales to near Chepstow in Gwent. It was constructed by Offa, king of the English province called Mercia in the eighth century AD, to prevent attacks from the Welsh.

A very famous boundary mark is Hadrian's Wall, built by the Romans to keep the Scottish tribes out of Roman Britain. Hadrian's Wall was built in AD 122

▲ The ditch and two banks on these hills are the remains of Offa's Dyke, near Clun in Shropshire.

and runs for 117 km from Wallsend (in Newcastle-upon-Tyne) to Bowness in Cumbria.

Hedges, trees, banks, walls, streams, roads and rivers were common boundary marks between Saxon or medieval villages. Some hedges are very old. See how many different plants are in a hedge; the more it contains the older it is likely to be.

Wells and ponds

We often forget that people have been able to get water from taps for only the last hundred years. Prehistoric people had to fetch their water from springs, streams and ponds. The Romans made wells, by digging deep into the ground until they found water. Wells and pumps were the main sources of drinking water for most towns and villages until this century. You can still see wells and pumps on village greens or in the main street. There is a signpost combined with a pump at Dorking in Surrey, and an elaborate well at Abinger Common, Surrey.

Ponds had many purposes: watering animals, washing clothes, working iron, farming fish, and, later, for filling steam engines. They were also used for 'swimming' people suspected of being witches: those who floated were said to be guilty, those who drowned, innocent!

Some hollows in the ground that contain water were not intended as ponds. They are the results of mining minerals or digging clay. You may be able to see if this is the case by looking at an Ordnance Survey map.

There were ponds all over Britain's villages and fields, but sadly they are now disappearing. Ashmore in Dorset is one village that still has a lovely pond.

▼ Many villages probably grew up around ponds because they were such an important source of water before it was carried around in pipes. This pond has been preserved in the village of Finchingfield, Essex.

Industry

Early people mined flint and metals to make tools and weapons. Stone for buildings and roads was taken from quarries. Mills provided the power for machines until steam power was invented.

Mines

Prehistoric people used tools made of flint and other stone. Flint is a hard stone found in chalk hills, and the best flint is found about 12 m below the ground. Neolithic people mined this using picks made of bone or the antlers of deer. You can visit an actual Neolithic mine at

▼ There are 366 of these grass-covered hollows at Breckland, Norfolk. They are called Grimes Graves, and cover the shafts of mines where Neolithic people mined the flint they used for tools.

Grimes Graves in Norfolk. At Cissbury hillfort in Sussex you can see 200 or so depressions in the ground which are the remains of Neolithic mines. The mines are over 2,000 years older than the hillfort itself.

The first metal used was copper, which is made by heating certain types of stone. This was later combined with tin to make bronze, which is a stronger metal. Tin was mined in Cornwall until quite recently. You can still see

the spoil heaps of tin mines – the mounds of rock from which the tin was taken – around the Bodmin moors.

Iron, which has been used from the Iron Age onwards, is made by smelting: melting iron ore – rock containing iron – in ovens or furnaces. The ore was mined in pits of around 6 m deep and 2 m across. These bell pits can still be found in wooded country in the south of England as depressions in the ground, which are now often filled with water.

Lead, gold and coal have also been used since the Roman period. Lead was mined in Somerset, Wales, Derbyshire and Yorkshire. Silver is extracted from the same ores as lead. Lead was a major product in Roman times and again in the seventeenth and eighteenth centuries. Remains of lead mines can be seen at Laxey Wheel in the Isle of Man, and Killhope Lead Mill in Weardale, Durham. Roman gold mines can be visited at Dolaucothi in Dyfed, Wales.

The Romans probably didn't mine coal but took it from places where it showed in the rock surface. Coal has been mined in Britain since medieval times and you often see the remains of old coal workings: large waste tips, disused pits, air shafts, derelict canals and so on. The Big Pit mining museum of Blaenavon, Gwent, shows how coal was mined.

Quarries

In areas where there was no flint, early people made their tools from other stone. Early quarries can be seen at Great Langdale in the Lake District; near Cushendall, Antrim; and near Penzance in Cornwall. Quarries where stone and gravel have been extracted for building and road mending, perhaps since Roman times, are a

▲ An old slate quarry at Cwmorthen, near Blaenau Ffestiniog, Gwynedd. The mine shafts were deep inside the mountain. Slate was used for roofs, and for writing on. Quarrying for slate used to be a major industry in north Wales, but slate is no longer in great demand and so this quarry is now deserted.

common feature of the landscape. Many old gravel pits are now finding a new use as boating or fishing lakes.

Mills

Mills used power from water or wind to drive machinery, until the invention of engines powered by steam in the eighteenth century.

Water-mills, which were used in Roman times, are much older than windmills. Water from a stream turned the wheel of the mill which ground grain into flour or drove machines used for fulling (part of the woollen cloth making process). The water had to be running at just the right speed – fast enough to turn the wheel properly but not so fast that it damaged it. In Saxon and medieval times only the lord of the manor could own a mill, which all his tenants used to grind their grain. Later, water-mills were used for other industries like paper-making.

▼ This water-mill at Osmaston, Derbyshire, probably built in the 1840s, was used for sawing timber. The wheel was turned by water from a fast-running stream.

Project

Reconstructing the past
Think of a building or location from the past near your home. Or find a picture in a book of an interesting landmark. This could be the remains of a Roman villa; a cave where people lived in ancient times; an old railway line; the ruins of a castle, church or a windmill – to name just a few ideas.

Draw a picture of how you think this place looked at the time when people lived there or used it for its original purpose.

To make your picture as accurate as possible, try to find out:
* what sort of people lived there? Were they rich, poor, or did all sorts of different people live or work together?
* what sort of clothes did people wear? Is your picture set in winter or summer?
* what did the houses look like?
* what sort of food did people eat? Did they keep animals, or grow crops?

When you have drawn your picture, write a story about the people who lived there. You could imagine one complete day in the life of a family or a village, or you could write about what happens to one particular person in your drawing.

There are still many mills, or remains of mills, in Britain, and some are still working. Good water-mills to visit are Nether Alderley mill in Cheshire, and Headley mill in Bordon, Hampshire.

Windmills, powered by wind-driven sails which turn a wheel, date, in Britain, from the twelfth century. They were mainly used for grinding corn but also for sawing wood, making gunpowder and other things. Some medieval windmills were built on low mounds called tumps and many tumps still survive on their own even if the mill itself has gone. Tumps can easily be confused with small barrows (see page 38), so look for other medieval remains around them: ridge and furrow patterns (see page 24), old manor houses and churches. Some windmills have been converted into houses.

▲ All the machinery was removed from the windmill at Thorpeness, Suffolk, on the right of the picture, so that it could be used to pump water to the little house on the left. This house, built on top of an old water tower, is called 'The House in the Clouds'.

Sussex, Kent and East Anglia are the best counties in which to see complete windmills. Mills still working include North Leverton mill in Shropshire and Outwood mill in Surrey.

Worship

People have always worshipped gods in some form or another. Early people held meetings for religious or other ceremonies in large enclosures, often surrounded by big stones; later, people worshipped in temples and churches.

Henge monuments and stone circles

These are large circular enclosures, which were probably used for religious and other celebrations. Neolithic people started constructing them and they were used for 2,000 years (which is the same length of time that Christianity has been a religion).

Henge monuments consist of a high bank and a deep ditch with one or more entrances. Some of them are huge: the henge at Durrington Walls in Wiltshire covers more than 12 hectares of land. The flat area in the centre was probably the temple. Here, later Bronze Age people put up one or more massive

▲ The henge monument at Avebury, Wiltshire, was built about 4,500 years ago. It is one of the most spectacular Neolithic sites in Europe, and covers 12 hectares. The medieval village grew up right inside it. Originally there were 600 stones, but only 76 now remain.

stone circles (like the famous henges of Avebury and Stonehenge in Wiltshire), or enormous wooden structures. Unlike prehistoric monuments built for defence, the bank of a henge is usually outside the ditch. Did people sit on this to watch the ceremonies in the temple area? Some henge monuments have rows of stones leading away from them. These may have been avenues, used for processions.

There are many smaller, simpler stone circles without a bank and ditch, particularly in Scotland and Ireland. Some, like Boscawen-Un in Cornwall, have one large stone in the centre of the circle. We don't know what this was used for, but it may have been to help prehistoric people plot the rising and setting of the sun at different times of the year. Good examples of stone circles are Castlerigg, Cumbria; Rollright Stones, Oxfordshire; Callanish, Isle of Lewis; and Drombohilly, County Kerry.

You sometimes see large stones (called monoliths or menhirs) standing on their own. These probably date from the Bronze Age, and may have been memorials to a dead person, statues to a god, or boundary marks.

Temples

As well as stone circles, Neolithic and Bronze Age people probably used the entrances to megalithic tombs (see page 38) as temples. Iron Age people built wooden temples – one was found when Heathrow airport was being built (it's right under Runway One!) – but none of these survive today. Roman temples were often made of stone, and good examples are at Carrawburgh on Hadrian's Wall in Northumberland, Littlecote in Oxfordshire and Queen Victoria Street, London.

▼ The White Horse at Uffington, Berkshire, possibly the symbol of an Iron Age tribe.

Hill figures

The huge pictures of horses, giants and other things you see cut into the chalk hills of southern England are like early examples of graffiti! They are impossible to date, but many were made in the 1700s and later. Three hill figures which are known to be much older (Iron Age, Roman, Saxon or medieval) are the White Horse at Uffington (Berkshire), the Cerne Abbas Giant (Dorset) and the Long Man of Wilmington (Sussex). These might have been the emblems of a particular tribe or might have had something to do with pre-Christian ceremonies or festivals.

◄ This Celtic cross is at Monasterboice, Co Louth, Ireland. It dates from the ninth or tenth century AD, and is decorated with scenes from the Bible. Priests often held services beside a cross if there was no church nearby.

Crosses

Tall, upright, Christian crosses are some of the most common monuments to be seen in Britain. The earliest are Celtic crosses, dating from the seventh century AD, which have a circle round the middle of the cross. They are often decorated with birds, plants, scenes from the Bible, or abstract designs.

In the medieval period, crosses were put up in many places: by roadsides, at crossroads, on village greens, in market places and in churchyards. They were used as places to preach from, and traders sold their goods around their bases.

Churches

Some churches appear to have been built on the sites of earlier, non-Christian places of worship. Large standing stones are often found in churchyards, and the churches at Knowlton in Dorset, and Midmar, Scotland, are right in the middle of henge monuments or Bronze Age stone circles.

The church was the centre of village life in medieval times, and would usually have been in the middle of the village or on the main street. If you see a church that is some way away from the village, this may be because the village became smaller or moved from its original position.

Abbeys and priories

Although Christianity came to Britain during the Roman period, Britain didn't really become a Christian country until later Saxon times. From around AD 600, monks and nuns from Europe started to establish religious communities in Britain (called monasteries and convents). These became very important during the medieval years when most of the abbeys and priories, where the monks and nuns lived, were built. As well as places of learning (the monks and nuns were among the few people in Britain who could read or write), the abbeys and priories owned a great deal of land and became very rich.

▲ Bolton Abbey in Yorkshire was founded in 1155. After 1540 it fell into ruins.

King Henry VIII closed down the abbeys and priories between 1524 and 1540, and took their possessions. Some of the monastic churches became the cathedrals we know today (Westminster Abbey, St Albans Cathedral); others became parish churches (Tewkesbury, Gloucestershire; Hexham, Northumberland). Many abbeys and priories, though, were abandoned altogether. Their remains can often be seen. Beautiful old abbeys are Fountains in Yorkshire and Tintern in Gwent.

Burial

The way people are buried has always been an important part of their religion. Early people put up large mounds of earth or stone over their dead; people today mark burial places with a gravestone.

Since the Neolithic period, monuments have been put up to the dead, and religious ceremonies held around these burial places.

Archaeological investigations have shown that people were often buried wearing their best clothes and jewellery, and with objects such as knives, swords and buckets. Sometimes remains of food have been found with the body, as well as dogs, horses, chariots and boats – even slaves and wives. These may have been placed with the body to help the spirit on its journey to, or during, the next life. It was quite common, from Roman times, to put a coin on the eyes or mouth of a dead person, to pay for the journey into the world of the dead. Burial sites are therefore very important to archaeologists, as they tell us a lot about the lives and customs of early people.

Bodies were sometimes cremated (burnt) rather than buried. Cremation went in and out of fashion as a way of disposing of bodies until the eighth century AD. It was then forbidden by the Christian church, and no bodies were cremated again until the nineteenth century.

▶ The funeral of the Saxon King of East Anglia may have looked like this. His grave at Sutton Hoo contained a large boat, weapons, jewellery and other possessions. Slaves may also have been killed and buried nearby.

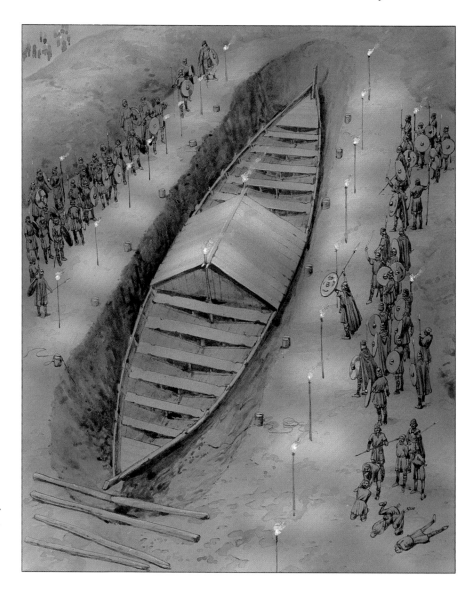

When bodies were cremated, the body would be burnt on a wooden pyre at the burial site and the ashes placed in a pot, called an urn. When the body was not cremated, it was often left to decompose on a wooden table before being placed in the burial mound, probably to allow time for the spirit to leave the body. Sometimes the head was cut from the body and buried between the legs or in another place altogether. This may have been intended to stop the corpse coming back as a ghost.

Long barrows

These are large mounds, usually on top of hills, where the first (Neolithic) farmers buried their dead. They usually measure from 20 to 125 metres long and 1 to 7 metres high. The width is normally between one quarter and half their length. They are normally higher and wider at one end (usually the east) and this is where the bodies are buried.

Long barrows have wooden burial chambers and usually contain many bodies, perhaps all members of one important family or tribe. The bodies were probably collected together over a period of time and placed under the mound in a single ceremony.

Over 200 of these long barrows can still be seen, mainly on the chalk hills of Wiltshire (particularly near the stone circles of Stonehenge and Avebury); the North and South Downs in Surrey and Sussex; the Chilterns in Berkshire/Oxfordshire/Buckinghamshire. There are also long barrows in East Anglia, Lincolnshire and East Yorkshire. A good example of a long barrow is

▲ Belas Knapp, Gloucestershire. A Neolithic long barrow covering a megalithic tomb with stone chambers for the burials. Ceremonies probably took place at the entrance to these tombs.

near the crossroads of the A303 and A360 at Winterbourne Stoke in Wiltshire.

Many long barrows were made of chalk. These are now covered with grass, but they must have been quite a sight when first built: enormous mounds of pure white chalk surrounded by deep ditches from which the earth for the mound had been dug.

Landmarks from the Past

Megalithic tombs

Built around the same time as the long barrows, but mainly in the west of Britain, these are barrows with stone chambers for the burials. (Megalith means a large stone; tomb means a house for the dead.) The entrance to the tomb was made up of several massive stones and, unlike the long barrows, could be reopened to allow more bodies to be added from time to time.

Most megalithic tombs were originally covered with large mounds, some round, some sausage-shaped, so that at first glance it can be difficult to tell a megalithic stone-chambered tomb from a long barrow with wooden chambers. If it has an entrance with several large stones it is a megalithic tomb. However, the mounds have disappeared from many megalithic tombs and only the stone chamber remains. This is called a dolmen, and a good example is Kit's Coty House, near Aylesford, Kent.

Around 2,000 megalithic tombs can still be seen in Britain and Ireland. Some good examples are Maes Howe on the Island of Orkney; West Kennet, near Avebury, Wiltshire; Wayland's Smithy, Berkshire; Belas Knapp, near Winchcombe, Gloucestershire; Bryn Celli Ddu, Anglesey; Newgrange in County Meath, Ireland.

Round barrows

The fashion for burying a number of people in one large mound died out in the Bronze Age. After this, smaller mounds, usually round, were put up over the body of one, or sometimes more, important people.

Most round barrows were built in the Bronze Age, but there are some Iron Age barrows, particularly in Yorkshire and Humberside. Some of these have square ditches surrounding them. The Romans also built some

▼ Kit's Coty House, near Aylesford, Kent, the burial chamber of a Neolithic megalithic tomb. It was once covered by a mound but this has now disappeared. Burial rites must have been important to the first farmers, judging by the size of the monuments they put up.

▲ There are over 260 of these Bronze Age burial mounds, or round barrows, around Stonehenge in Wiltshire, and they are often found in groups. The path on the left is called the Ridgeway and was a main trackway for prehistoric people.

ploughing, show up on aerial photographs from the ditches which surrounded them. To find round barrows, look on an Ordnance Survey map for the word tumulus or tumuli (tumuli means there are several barrows in the same spot). Good areas for barrow-hunting are the chalk hills from Dorset to Berkshire and the moorlands of north-east Yorkshire.

Cairns

Mounds of stones were placed over burial places in the mountainous country of Wales and Scotland during the Bronze Age and Iron Age. A good example of a burial cairn is Camster Long at Watten in Scotland.

Not all cairns are early burial sites. They may simply be heaps of stones removed by farmers from a field, sight marks for laying out tracks, or just markers for a boundary between one area and another.

Bronze Age and Iron Age burials were often contained in boxes of stone slabs called cists. These are sometimes found under cairns and barrows, as well as on their own without a mound.

barrows. Good examples are the three large, steep, cone-shaped barrows known as the Bartlow Hills in the village of Bartlow, Cambridgeshire.

The Saxons sometimes raised small mounds over burials, and larger barrows were built for some royal or very important people, the most interesting being the group of seventeen at Sutton Hoo in Suffolk, one of which contained treasures of gold and silver and a large boat. In Iron Age and Saxon times, the dead were also placed in the sides of Bronze Age barrows.

There are many thousands of round barrows still to be seen all over Britain. Many more, where the mounds have been destroyed by

Cemeteries

There are Bronze Age cemeteries where many barrows are found in the same place. A good example is the Seven Barrows at Lambourn, Berkshire, although its name is misleading since there were over 40 barrows here. There are Iron Age cist grave cemeteries at Danby Rigg, Yorkshire, where 800 cist burials were found. Burial under the ground without a mound became normal practice at the end of the Iron Age.

The Romans built large cemeteries along the roads leading out of the main towns and forts. Saxon cemeteries are occasionally found by archaeologists, but when Britain became a fully Christian country in the eighth century AD, people were buried in churches and churchyards.

However, by the end of the 1700s the churchyards were getting overcrowded. Graves were reused to save space, which is why the floors of older churches are often lower than the ground outside. Finding space to bury people became such a problem that an Act of Parliament allowed separate cemeteries, away from churches, to be developed at the end of the nineteenth century. One of the largest of these is Brookwood, near Woking in Surrey, set up by the London Necropolis Company. It originally had its own railway station in London connecting with two stations at the

▲ This cemetery in Hove, Sussex, opened in 1882. From the 1850s, if the churchyards were too full, local governments had to find more land for burials.

cemetery, and there are special burial areas for people of different religions, different nationalities and different professions.

Gravestones

Markers, placed at the head of a grave and engraved with the name of the person who had died, were introduced by the Romans, who called them *stelae*. There are no Roman gravestones in Christian churchyards, but you can see them in museums. There are also some Saxon and Norman gravestones in museums. Viking tombstones, known as hogbacks, dating from the tenth century, can be found in some churchyards. They are shaped and decorated as imitation houses. You can find them at Penrith and Crosscanonby in Cumbria, for instance, and inside the church at Govan, Glasgow.

However, it wasn't until the eighteenth century that it became common for people to have something to mark their grave. These markers were usually made of stone, but wood, iron and slate were (and still are) used as well. It can be very interesting to walk round a graveyard and read the writing on the gravestones. Some early ones are quite unusual. Here is one from a child's grave in a Suffolk churchyard: 'Came in. Walked about. Didn't like it. Walked out.'

There are also grander monuments in churchyards: big tombs and statues, particularly of angels. Extremely wealthy people, starting with the Romans, built very large tombs, sometimes as big as a house, called mausoleums. These are found in the grounds of stately homes (a very good example is at Castle Howard, Yorkshire) as well as in churchyards.

▼ These very old twin-headed gravestones from the Cotswolds probably mark the grave of a married couple.

Project

Exploring a graveyard
Visit your local cemetery or churchyard. Take a pen and paper with you.

1 Take 20 gravestones, and write down the names, dates and details of the people who are buried in the graves.
2 How old were they when they died?
3 What was the average age at which these people died? (Add up all the ages, and divide them by the number of gravestones you have looked at – in this case, 20.)
4 How many people with the same name can you find?
5 What is the most interesting saying or quotation on a headstone?
6 Draw the gravestone you like best, and explain why you like it.

Glossary

AD The years after the birth of Christ. AD is an abbreviation of the Latin words *Anno Domini*, which mean 'the year of the Lord'.

Aqueduct A structure like a bridge which carries water over a piece of lower ground.

Archaeological excavation Digging into the ground to find evidence of how people lived in the past.

Arctic The ice-covered region at the North Pole.

BC Means 'before Christ' and is used to describe the centuries and years before Christ's birth. The years number backwards, so 1000 BC is much earlier than 100 BC.

Barrow A large mound of earth under which people were buried in prehistoric times.

Boundary A line which divides areas of land belonging to different people, or different countries.

Bronze Age The years between 2500 BC and 600 BC, when people learned how to make tools from the metal bronze, a combination of copper and tin.

Celts Celtic people came from western and central Europe, and lived in Britain during the Iron Age.

Cremation Disposal of dead bodies by burning, rather than by burial in the ground.

Enclosure The process of dividing and fencing open, common land by wealthy landowners, which occurred in Britain mainly between 1740 and 1850. Before then, most country people had been able to use land for grazing animals and growing crops. After enclosure, many people were cut off from their way of making a living, or had to pay money to use the land.

Flint A hard stone which forms sharp pieces when it is broken. It was one of the first materials used to make tools and weapons.

Iron Age The years from 600 BC to AD 43 when iron was first used to make weapons and tools.

Medieval period The period in British history which lasted from 1066 to 1485.

Mesolithic period The time between about 10,000 BC and 4000 BC, when people in Britain made stone stools and weapons using small flakes of flint, sometimes set in bone or wooden handles.

Mill A building fitted with machinery for grinding. Early mills were driven by wind or water. They ground grains for flour, made gunpowder and drove machinery.

Mine A hole dug in the earth, for taking out minerals such as copper, iron, coal or salt. Mines can either be tunnels under the ground, or big, open holes. The process of taking out the minerals is called mining.

Moat An area of water surrounding a house or castle, originally designed to keep unwanted people out. Moats were also used as places to store water and keep fish.

Mosaic A pattern of tiles of different shapes and colours, used as a floor covering in Roman times.

Neolithic period The years from about 4000 BC to 2500 BC when people learned how to cultivate wild cereal grasses for food and how to keep animals. This meant they could live in one place all the time.

Nomads People who move around from place to place, to look for animals or plants for food.

Palaeolithic period The years from about 1,000,000 BC to 10,000 BC when the first people came to live in Britain, probably from Europe. These people were hunters, and made simple tools of wood and stone.

Plough A tool for cutting furrows in soil, so that crops can be planted. Early ploughs were made of wood, and were pulled by oxen or horses.

Prehistoric A general word referring to the period before history was written down. In Britain this goes up to AD 43, the beginning of the Roman period.

Quarry A place where stone is dug out of the ground.

Roman period The years from AD 43 to AD 410, when Britain was part of the Roman Empire. The Romans came from Italy, and the empire stretched from Egypt to Scotland.

Saxons People from northern Europe who invaded Britain in the fourth and fifth centuries AD. They set up their own kingdoms, which eventually became England. The Saxon period lasted from AD 410 to 1066.

Turves Lumps of grass (including the roots and soil it grows in), cut out of the ground and used for building roofs, walls or mounds.

Viaduct A long structure like a bridge for carrying a road or a railway over a valley.

Vikings Warriors and traders from Norway, Sweden and Denmark who raided and settled in Britain in the eighth to eleventh centuries AD.

Places to Visit

England

SALISBURY PLAIN, WILTSHIRE: In quite a small area you can see: Stonehenge and Avebury (henge monuments with a stone circle); Woodhenge (a henge monument with its original wooden circle marked out); Silbury Hill (the largest mound made by prehistoric people – but nobody knows why); West Kennet Long Barrow and many round and other barrows.

MAIDEN CASTLE, DORSET: Iron Age hillfort. An earlier (Neolithic) causewayed camp lies below the hill-fort and surrounds the remains of a Roman temple.

HADRIAN'S WALL, NORTHUMBERLAND: Roman wall and forts.

CHESTER, CHESHIRE: Remains of a Roman amphitheatre; well-preserved medieval walls following the line of the Roman walls; cathedral dating from the eleventh century, which was originally an abbey – look at the carvings on the choir stalls; the 'Rows' – shops on two levels dating from the medieval period.

PORTCHESTER, HAMPSHIRE: Walls of a Roman fort built to defend the coast against Saxon raiders. Inside are the remains of a medieval castle and a twelfth-century church which was once part of a priory.

DOVER, KENT: A Roman 'painted house'; the remains of the only Roman lighthouse in Britain; medieval castle dating from the twelfth century.

YORK, YORKSHIRE: Tower from a Roman fortress; 'Jorvik Viking Centre' – re-creation of York in Viking times; cathedral dating from the thirteenth century; two 'mottes' built by William the Conqueror, one with a thirteenth-century keep (Clifford's Tower); medieval walls and remains of thirteenth-century abbey.

Wales

CAERLEON, NR NEWPORT, GWENT: Roman fort and town with Legionary Museum, remains of Roman barracks, walls, theatre, and the most complete Roman baths to be found in Britain.

NEVERN, DYFED: Remains of a Norman motte and bailey castle and a stone castle. Three km to the south is Pentre Ifan Neolithic burial cairn; and 3 km to the south-east is Castell Henllys, an Iron Age hillfort.

Scotland

ORKNEY ISLANDS: Skara Brae Neolithic stone village; Maes Howe Neolithic burial cairn (also contains Viking carvings); Ring of Brogar Bronze Age stone circle.

SHETLAND ISLES: Remains of Bronze Age, Iron Age (wheelhouses) and Viking houses at Jarlshof, near Sumburgh Head; Iron Age broch on Mousa Island.

Northern Ireland

OMAGH, CO TYRONE: Ulster History Park. The history of Ireland told by reconstructed buildings and monuments, including Mesolithic and Neolithic huts, a megalithic tomb, a fort, and a motte and bailey castle.

Ireland

BOYNE VALLEY, CO MEATH AND CO LOUTH: Several fine megalithic burial chambers with stone passages, particularly those at Newgrange, Dowth and Knowth. Ruined abbeys of Bective, Mellifort and Monasterboice.

Books to Read

Bolwell, L and Lines, C, *The Countryside in the Past* (Wayland, 1987)

Cork, B and Reid, S, *Archaeology*, Young Scientist Series (Usborne, 1984)

Garnett, R, *The Story of Britain* (Harper Collins, 1991)

Gee, R and Evans, M A, *Usborne Guide to Britain* (Usborne, 1977)

Hamey, L A and J A, *The Roman Engineers* (Topic Books, CUP, 1985)

Marsden, Barry M, *Prehistoric Britain*, History in Evidence Series (Wayland, 1989)

O'Connell, Martin, *Roman Britain*, History in Evidence Series (Wayland, 1989)

Place, R, *Clues from the Past* (Wayland, 1993) *Medieval Britain*, History in Evidence Series (Wayland, 1989)

Sauvain, P, *Britain's Living Heritage* (Batsford, 1982)

Triggs, Tony D, *Norman Britain,* History in Evidence Series (Wayland, 1990) *Saxon Britain*, History in Evidence Series (Wayland, 1989)

Index

Page numbers in **bold** refer to illustrations as well as text.